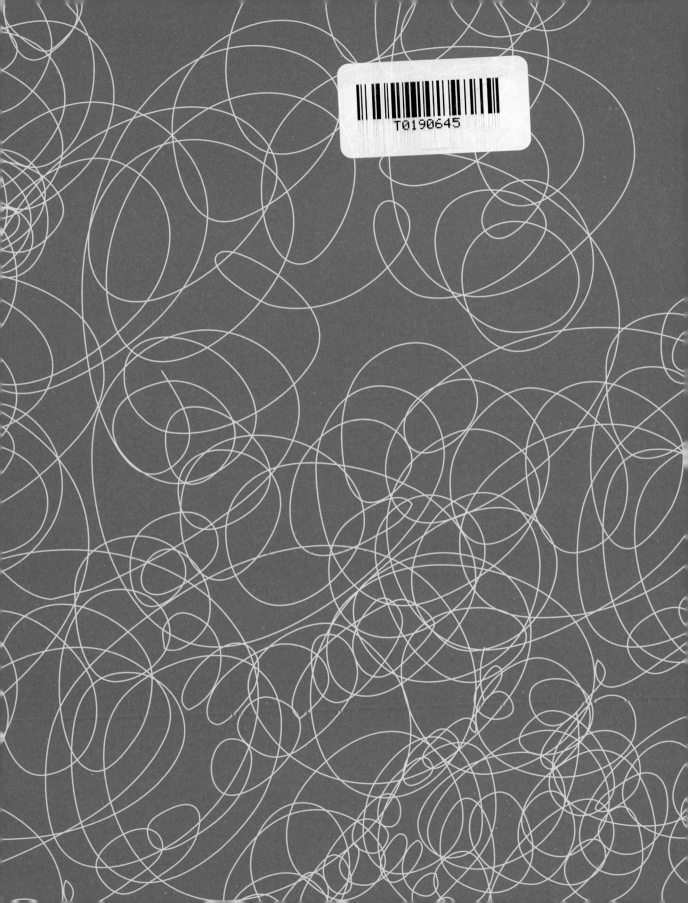

Usborne

ARCHITECTURE

Scribble Book

THE BUILDINGS IN THIS BOOK WERE SCRIBBLED BY:

Written by
EDDIE REYNOLDS &
DARRAN STOBBART

Illustrated by
PETRA BAAN

Designed by
Samuel Gorham
& Emily Barden

Series editor **Rosie Dickins**

Series designer **Zoe Wray**

Expert advice from
PROFESSOR SHANNON CHANCE

CONTENTS

Discover architectural styles old and new.

Design a shelter using limited materials.

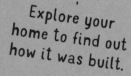

Explore your home to find out how it was built.

Draw a castle so safe no invader could break in.

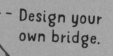

Design your own bridge.

Where would you build your dream home?

WHAT IS ARCHITECTURE?

Architecture is the process of DESIGNING and CONSTRUCTING buildings –
whether that's a room, a house or an entire city.
Architecture is done by ARCHITECTS.

Often architects design
new buildings from scratch...

...but they also repair, adapt and
improve existing buildings.

BEFORE AFTER

BEFORE AFTER

Most architects are trained to design ANY kind
of building. But some go on to SPECIALIZE in a
particular TYPE of architecture, such as...

Gardens

LANDSCAPE ARCHITECTURE:
Outdoor spaces.

Parks

Factories

Power
plants

INDUSTRIAL ARCHITECTURE:
Big industrial buildings,
such as factories.

Warehouses

Solar-powered
buildings

GREEN ARCHITECTURE:
Buildings that are
environmentally friendly.

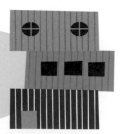

Tiny houses

Buildings made of
reused materials

To make buildings PRACTICAL and SAFE, architects have to think like an
ENGINEER. To make buildings LOOK GOOD, they have to think like an ARTIST.

WHAT'S IN THIS BOOK?

Before setting foot on a building site, most architects begin by scribbling ideas and designs on paper. This book is full of things to...

Imagine

DESIGN

BUILD

TEST

SOLVE

WHAT WILL YOU NEED?

For most of the book, you'll only need a pencil. Occasionally you might need glue or clear sticky tape, a ruler and scissors.

USBORNE QUICKLINKS

To download copies of the templates in this book, and for links to websites with more architecture facts and activities, go to **usborne.com/Quicklinks** and type in the keywords: **scribble architecture**. Please follow the internet safety guidelines at Usborne Quicklinks. Children should be supervised online.

THINK LIKE AN ARCHITECT

Imagine you could create any building you wanted.

WHAT WOULD YOU BUILD?

Pick one of these ideas,
or scribble your own.

House

Palace

Hotel

I'D LIKE TO BUILD:

Now answer the following questions to help you plan your building.
This process is known as **STRATEGIC DEFINITION.**

WHERE WILL IT BE?

Suggest a few places where you might want
your building to be located, then pick one.

Up a mountain?

In a city?

By the sea?

Often, architects are HIRED
by somebody to design a
building. The person hiring
usually chooses the type of
building and location.

WHAT'S GOOD?

Write down the ADVANTAGES of your chosen location, and ways your building could make the most of them.

Amazing views

Rooms with balconies?

Big windows?

Storage space for surfing equipment?

Near a beach

Shop selling beach kit?

WHAT'S NOT SO GOOD?

Unfortunately, any location will come with DISADVANTAGES, too. Think of some, along with ways your building could overcome them.

Fireplace in every room?

Cold winters

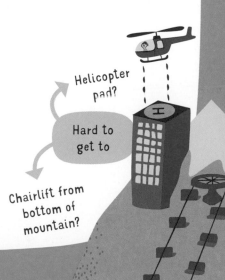

Helicopter pad?

Hard to get to

Chairlift from bottom of mountain?

A cyclist

Secure place to keep bicycles

Changing rooms

Showers

Somewhere to refill water bottles

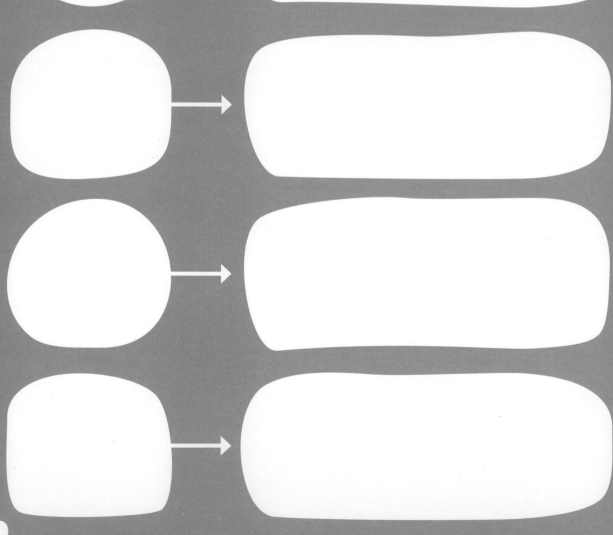

DRAW LIKE AN ARCHITECT

Once you've worked out what your building needs, it's time to DRAW it.
This is known as CONCEPT DESIGN. Follow the steps to help you
draw the building you've just planned.

Scribble a few ROUGH SKETCHES
to show what it might look like
from the outside. Architects do
this quickly to test ideas.

Don't think about details, such
as the layout of the rooms.
Just sketch the basic shape
of the building and the
nearby surroundings.

Some architects call this the
TWO-MINUTE SKETCH stage,
because each sketch should
take two minutes or less.

STEP 2: Make a FLOORPLAN. That's like a flat MAP of a building, drawn from a bird's-eye view. It helps an architect work out the shape and layout of the rooms.

Here's a floorplan of a guest house, with the different rooms marked.

Architects use SYMBOLS to represent different things in a plan. Find out what each symbol means below.

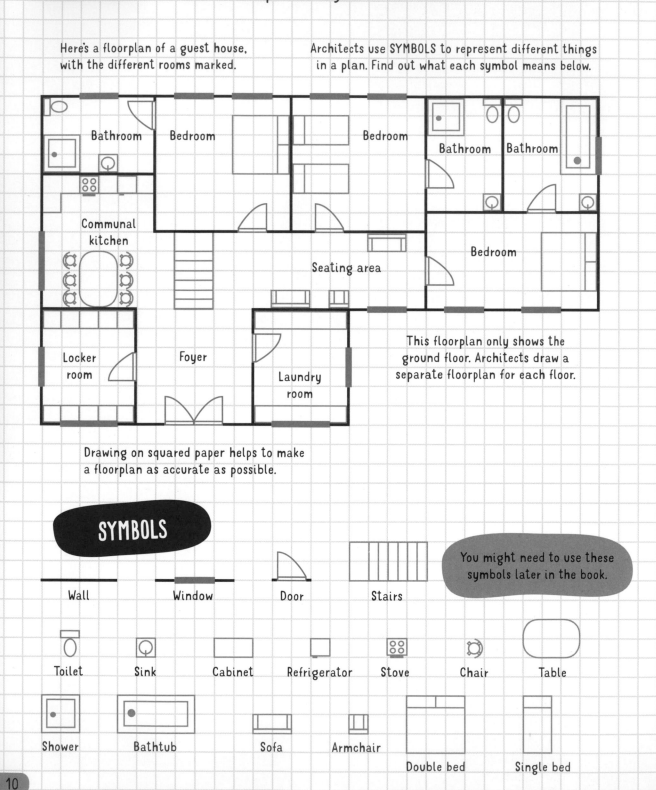

Bathroom
Bedroom
Bedroom
Bathroom
Bathroom
Communal kitchen
Seating area
Bedroom
Locker room
Foyer
Laundry room

This floorplan only shows the ground floor. Architects draw a separate floorplan for each floor.

Drawing on squared paper helps to make a floorplan as accurate as possible.

SYMBOLS

You might need to use these symbols later in the book.

Wall
Window
Door
Stairs

Toilet
Sink
Cabinet
Refrigerator
Stove
Chair
Table

Shower
Bathtub
Sofa
Armchair
Double bed
Single bed

DRAW your floorplan using the symbols from the previous page.

You could draw floorplans for one or two floors.

INVENT symbols for anything extra you want to include.

STEP 3:

A **FRONT ELEVATION** is a straight-on view showing the front of a building. Draw one for your building.

THINK...

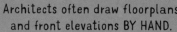

Is the entrance easy to find?

How many floors will it have?

What shape is the roof?

Have you included your ideas from pages 6-11?

Architects often draw floorplans and front elevations BY HAND.

The next stages are 3-D drawings, which are more complicated. They're usually done on a computer.

This is known as COMPUTER-AIDED DESIGN, or CAD. It saves architects a lot of time, and is more ACCURATE than drawing by hand.

12

BRICKWORK

Bricks are rectangular blocks of baked clay, used for building. They're popular with architects because they're strong, hard-wearing and can be used to make walls of all shapes and sizes. Bricks are usually arranged to make patterns.

Staggered rows of bricks are known as RUNNING BOND.

This pattern is known as BASKETWEAVE.

This zigzag pattern is called HERRINGBONE.

This is very common because it's strong and easy to make.

It looks nice, but it's not as strong as running bond.

It's strong AND decorative.

Look out for these patterns in the buildings you pass by.

SKETCH OUT a decorative design for a brick wall.

IDEAS

Bricks come in lots of different shades.

You could turn the bricks around so that they're sideways.

Your design could have holes to let light through...

...or gaps for people to sit in.

WINDOWS

An architect has to decide the SHAPE, SIZE and POSITION of every window in a building. Below are some different types of windows, and reasons why an architect might choose them.

It's relatively quick, easy and cheap to make RECTANGULAR frames and openings...

...but it's possible to make windows in almost ANY shape. Unusual-shaped windows can make a building look unique.

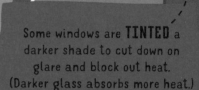

Some windows are **TINTED** a darker shade to cut down on glare and block out heat. (Darker glass absorbs more heat.)

A **PICTURE WINDOW** doesn't usually open. It's just a large sheet of glass that lets in lots of LIGHT and gives wide VIEWS.

FROSTED glass is harder to see through, so it's good for privacy.

A **SKYLIGHT** is a window set into a roof. It lets in extra LIGHT and, when open, lets out HEAT.

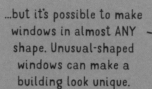

La la la, singing in the shower...

A **BAY WINDOW** sticks out from the wall. This lets in extra LIGHT, and gives a wider VIEW.

A **TRANSOM** is a window above a door. When open, it keeps the building VENTILATED, which means air can flow in and out easily.

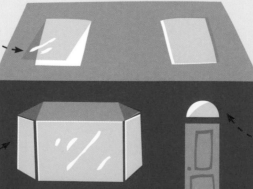

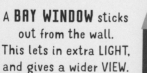

SCRIBBLE windows onto these buildings. Try to make them suitable for each building's needs.

APARTMENT BUILDING: - - - -
Needs lots of light, wide views, and privacy in bathrooms.

OFFICE BUILDING: Needs a variety of shapes to make it look different to the buildings around it, without becoming too bright or hot inside.

GROCERY STORE:
Needs to be well ventilated, and easy to see into from outside.

Fatima's **FOODS**

STRIKING STYLES

Certain STYLES of architecture become popular at different times.
Read the descriptions below and see if you can match each building to its style.

☐ **CLASSICAL** buildings have rows of tall, slim columns. Their roofs slope gently, often forming a triangle shape above the entrance.

☐ **MODERNIST** architecture has simple, blocky shapes and no decoration. It tends to use modern materials such as concrete, steel and glass.

☐ **ROCOCO** architecture has lots of decoration and curved features. Sometimes the outside of a building is painted or even covered in gold to make it sparkle.

☐ **ROMANESQUE** buildings have lots of rounded arches. They tend to have thick walls and small windows.

☐ **GOTHIC** buildings tend to be tall, with pointed arches. Extra supports, known as flying buttresses, often help to strengthen walls from the outside.

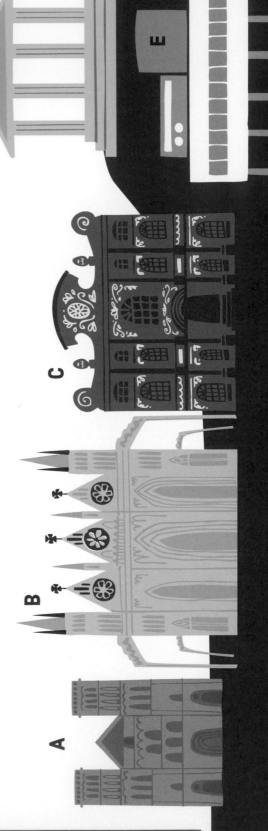

A

B

C

D

E

HOW WILL YOUR BUILDING LOOK?

WHAT WILL IT BE MADE OF?

Tall and narrow	Onion-shaped domes	Black and white	Glass and concrete	See-through plastic	Triangle-shaped blocks

INVENT your OWN style of architecture, then scribble a building in that style.

Your style could be ECLECTIC – which means it combines features from existing styles to create something new.

DOMES

DOMES have been a feature of architecture for THOUSANDS of years. But curved shapes are tricky to build, and early domes were made from heavy stone, so architects had to find clever ways to support them.

Filippo Brunelleschi designed a very wide dome for Florence Cathedral around 600 years ago.

Brunelleschi placed a large outer dome (shown in pink) over an inner one (shown in green).

Around 300 years ago, Sir Christopher Wren designed a dome (shown in pink) for St. Paul's cathedral.

The dome is supported by a hollow cone of bricks (shown in green).

The bricks are hidden on the inside by a smaller dome (shown in orange).

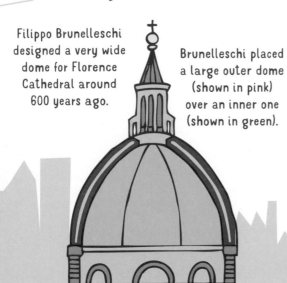

Modern building materials led to new types of curved structures – such as GEODESIC domes and roofs.

Geodesic structures use interlocking TRIANGLES to create lightweight but strong curved surfaces.

This geodesic roof was designed by Norman Foster in 2000 for the British Museum's Great Court. It contains 3,312 triangular panes of glass in a steel frame.

In his design, each triangle is a slightly different size and shape. A computer was used to calculate the size of each one.

BUILD A GEODESIC DOME

Copy this template, or download it from Usborne QUICKLINKS. Then follow the instructions on this page to create your own geodesic dome.

This dome is made of only TWO different shaped triangles.

Cut along the black lines.

Fold along the blue lines.

Use glue or clear sticky tape to secure the tabs.

Turn to the next page to see how your finished dome should look.

Your finished dome should look like this.

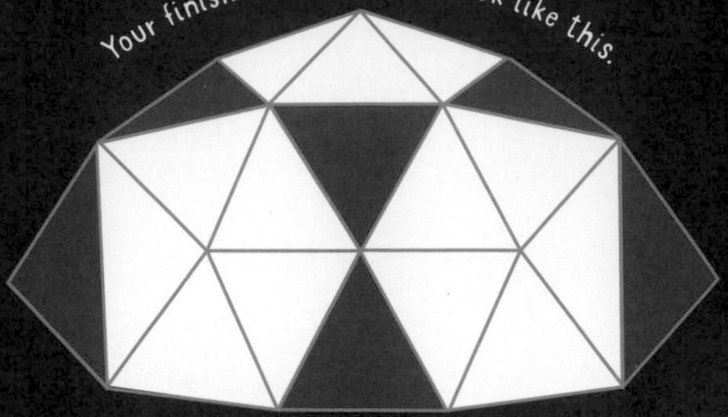

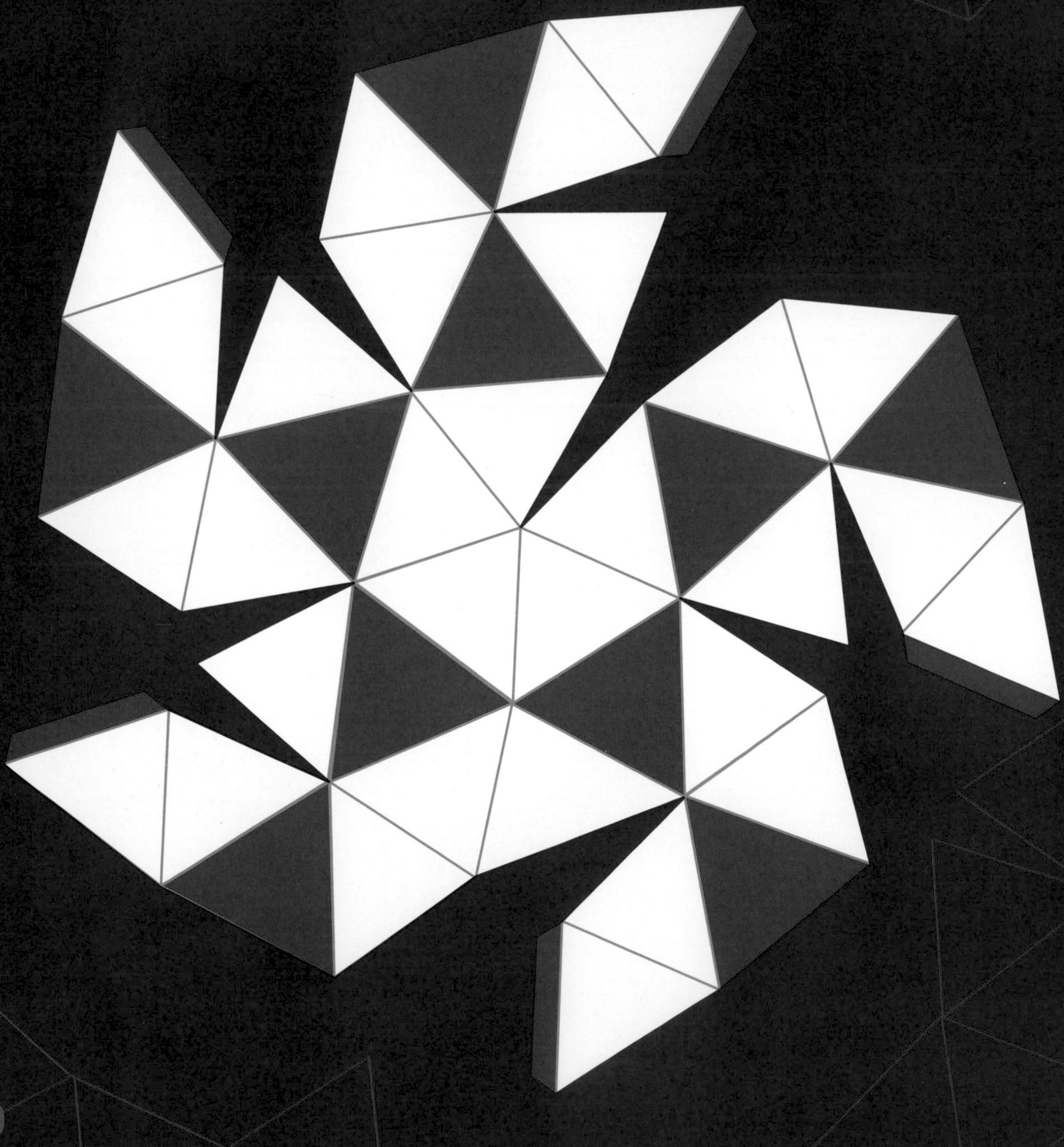

ICY DOMES

Hunters in the Arctic sometimes build domes out of snow, known as IGLOOS, to sleep in on hunting trips.

Igloo

The igloo below is being built with five special design features, to make it WARM and SAFE.

1 A thick wall that has been partly melted and REFROZEN into smooth, strong ice

2 An extra WALL around the igloo

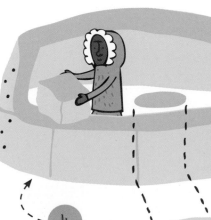

3 SMALL HOLES in the wall, poked through with a stick

4 A base no wider than 3m (10 feet) across

5 An UNDERGROUND TUNNEL as an entrance, instead of a big gap in the wall

Each of the features solves one of the problems below. Match each feature to the problem it solves.

A	B	C	D	E
STRONG WINDS and BLIZZARDS could blow an igloo down.	If the wall is thin or uneven, it might be WEAK and FALL IN.	If the dome is TOO WIDE it could collapse.	The hunter needs enough air to breathe.	If TOO MUCH air gets in, an igloo will become dangerously cold.

CREATING LANDSCAPES

People who design and create outdoor spaces, such as gardens and parks, are called LANDSCAPE ARCHITECTS.

Create your own bubble diagram for a PARK.

STEP 1:

Landscape architects begin by sketching a simple BUBBLE DIAGRAM to give a rough idea of where everything will go.

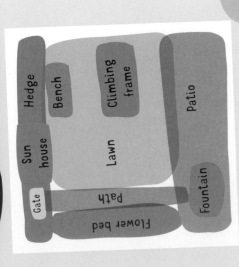

This is a bubble diagram for a back garden.

Hedge

Bench

Sun house

Climbing frame

Gate

Lawn

Path

Patio

Flower bed

Fountain

YOU COULD HAVE...

...a picnic area?

...a slide?

...swings?

...a running track?

STEP 2:

They then create a more detailed plan using SYMBOLS, to show exactly what will go where.

Turn your park bubble diagram into a more detailed plan, using the symbols below.

INVENT YOUR OWN symbols for anything else you want to include.

This is a plan of the garden above.

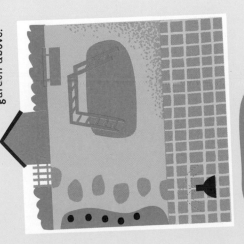

SYMBOLS

Building

Hedge

Fountain

Bench

Flower bed

Patio

Rocks

Climbing frame

NOT MUCH CHOICE

The earliest humans had to build shelters with whatever they could find – such as rocks, sticks and animal skins.

Here are some examples of materials, and how they were used.

VINES
USEFUL PROPERTIES:
Light, strong, flexible

Ropes to tie things together

ANIMAL SKINS
USEFUL PROPERTIES:
Waterproof, keep in heat

Roof or wall material

BRANCHES AND STICKS
USEFUL PROPERTIES:
Light, strong, sharp

Supports for the roof

Roof material

LONG GRASS AND LEAVES
USEFUL PROPERTIES:
Light, soft, keep in heat

ROCKS
USEFUL PROPERTIES:
Heavy, strong, keep in heat and release it to warm the inside

Walls

MUD
USEFUL PROPERTIES:
Easy to shape, hardens when dry, stores heat then releases it when surroundings cool

A way to stick things together

...for a WET and COLD place.

It needs to be
waterproof and
keep in heat.

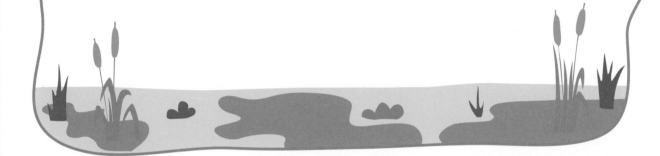

...for a WINDY place.

It needs to
be strong.

Leafy trees can
block cold winds.

Wind direction

A door facing AWAY
from the wind will let
in less cold air.

RESTORATIONS

Buildings can crumble over time, or be damaged in an accident.
Some architects use their skills to RESTORE damaged buildings and old ruins.

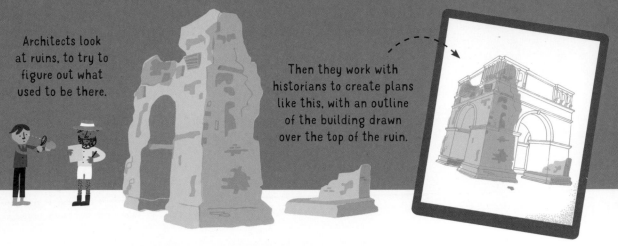

Architects look at ruins, to try to figure out what used to be there.

Then they work with historians to create plans like this, with an outline of the building drawn over the top of the ruin.

Some ruins can be restored using the original stones.

DRAW lines to match the blocks to the gaps in this crumbled ancient Greek temple.

A Chinese palace needs to be restored after a fire.
An architect has started the restoration plan below.

COMPLETE the unfinished plan.
The ruin is lightly shaded, and the
plan so far is shown in blue.

The palace was SYMMETRICAL –
meaning each side was a mirror
image of the other.

To keep your drawing
symmetrical, find a point
on the existing plan...

...count how many
squares it is from
the middle...

...then count the
same number along
on the other side.

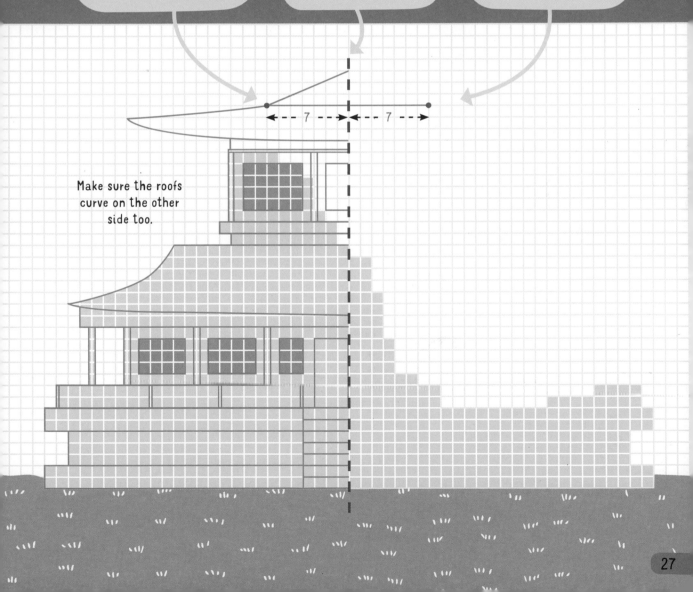

Make sure the roofs
curve on the other
side too.

INVESTIGATE YOUR HOME

Use these pages to record information about your home and discover some of the things the architect had to think about while designing it.

WHAT'S IT MADE OF? Look around the outside of your home for the materials below. What can you find where?

STONE OR BRICK	WOOD	PLASTIC	GLASS	METAL

THE WALLS

Most buildings have a few HOLLOW walls, containing pipes, wires and insulation. If you knock on a wall...

...A HOLLOW WALL
will make a DEEPER, LOUDER sound. It will also VIBRATE very slightly.

...A SOLID WALL
will make a QUIETER sound, and will hardly vibrate at all.

Pick a room to test.

ROOM:

Go inside the room and knock (gently) on each wall. How many sound hollow, and how many sound solid?

HOLLOW:

SOLID:

LIGHT AND DARK

How much light a room gets, and at what time of day, depends on which way its windows face.

Pick two rooms in your home to compare. On a clear day, mark when each of them is BRIGHTEST.

Try to pick rooms with an open view, so there's nothing to block the light.

ROOM 1:

ROOM 2:

BRIGHTEST: ○ ○ ○
Morning Afternoon Same all day

BRIGHTEST: ○ ○ ○
Morning Afternoon Same all day

WHICH WAY DO YOUR ROOMS FACE?

If a room is brightest in the MORNING, the windows must face roughly EAST, because that's where the Sun RISES.

If a room is the SAME ALL DAY, the windows must face NORTH or SOUTH. In places north of the equator, south-facing windows face the Sun all day. In places south of the equator, it's the other way around.

If a room is brightest in the AFTERNOON, the windows must face roughly WEST, because the Sun SETS in the west.

Architects often place bedrooms facing east, so they're brightest when you wake up.

Artists' studios often face AWAY from the Sun. This gives a steady light, without strong shadows.

West-facing windows are good in rooms that get used most in the afternoon and evening.

WEIRD AND WONDERFUL

Some architects are famous for creating unconventional designs – often creating bright and vibrant buildings in unusual shapes.

Austrian-born architect Friedensreich Hundertwasser's design tricks include...

(1928-2000)

(1852-1926)

Spanish architect Antoni Gaudí had many signature techniques...

Plants

No repetition

Spires

Wavy lines

Curvy, patterned chimneys

Mismatched windows

Ridged rooftops

Overhanging rooms and balconies

Tiles in many bright shades

Unusually shaped windows

Hundertwasser REALLY disliked straight lines. He once said...

"THE STRAIGHT LINE LEADS TO THE DOWNFALL OF HUMANITY!"

Archways and columns

IT COULD BE...

SCRIBBLE eye-catching designs on the blank structures below, and fill in the gap with an unusual building of your own.

A building made of mirrors?

A skyscraper that twists?

A building shaped like a ball?

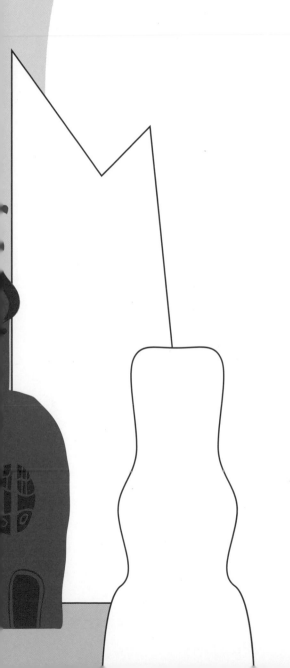

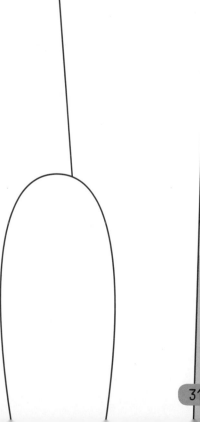

FLOOD ZONE

In places that are close to sea level, or have very heavy RAINFALL, buildings may get FLOODED. Architects in those places study the risk and design buildings that can withstand flooding.

This FLOOD ZONE MAP shows how likely different areas are to flood.

KEY:

- High-risk zone
- Medium-risk zone
- Low-risk zone
- Not considered at risk

Fisherman's Hill

Ship Creek

Crab Corner

Ferry Approach

Lighthouse Lane

Crab Street

Cliffside Way

Sail End

Coral Crescent

Shell Street

Pebble Road

Oyster Lane

Jellyfish Drive

Queen's Bridge

Barnacle Boulevard

Tidal Turn

Three people are having new homes constructed. Rank the flood risk of each location from 1 (lowest) to 3 (highest).

NEW HOME:
Cliffside Way
RANK: 1 / 2 / 3

NEW HOME:
Crab Street
RANK: 1 / 2 / 3

NEW HOME:
Pebble Road
RANK: 1 / 2 / 3

SCRIBBLE a design for a home in a high-risk flood zone. There are some ideas below for making it flood-proof.

YOU COULD ADD...

Rubber seals around doors

Stilts to raise it

Floating foundation

Pumps and pipes to get water out

Rooms that start higher up

SCALE DRAWINGS

Architects obviously can't draw buildings full-size – the plans would never fit on a piece of paper. Instead, architects SHRINK all the measurements by the same amount to make an accurate SCALE drawing.

This is a scale drawing of a museum café.

Scale: |— 1m —|

On this grid, each square is 1cm. The SCALE shows you that 1cm in the drawing represents 1m (100cm) in real life.

This particular scale can also be written as 1:100, because 1cm represents 100cm.

Kitchen

Café

This green wall is 6cm on the plan, so in real life it's 6m.

Bathroom

How long is the purple wall? ___ m

How long is the orange wall? ___ m

These museum exhibits are drawn to different scales. Can you calculate what size they are in real life?

You'll need a ruler.

For the first exhibit, the scale means 1cm is 40cm in real life.

The drawing is 5cm wide, so in real life, the exhibit is 5 x 40 = 200cm (or 2m) wide.

1:40

1:7

1:35

200 cm

___ cm

___ cm

The floorplan below shows a scale drawing of part of a museum. Add the exhibits below to the correct rooms.

A cabinet of hats through the ages
2½m x 1m

A life-size model triceratops
8m × 3m

A model of a Mars rover
3m × 2½m

A display of ancient jars
½m × 2m

Scale: 1m

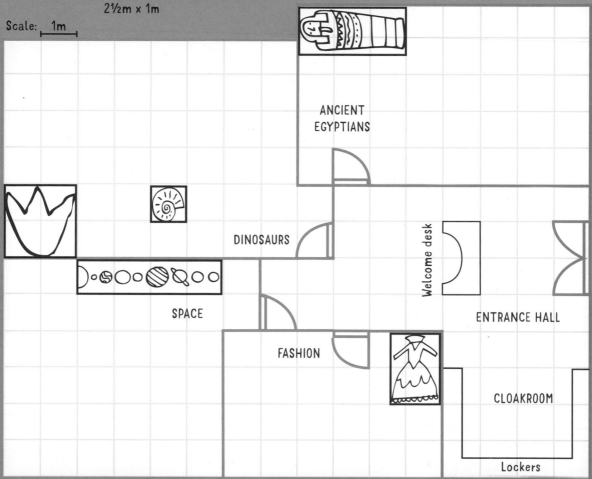

ANCIENT EGYPTIANS

DINOSAURS

SPACE

Welcome desk

ENTRANCE HALL

FASHION

CLOAKROOM

Lockers

After adding the exhibits, do you still have room for...

...a space rocket simulator
4m × 2½m?

YES / NO

...a sphinx statue
4m × 2m?

YES / NO

...a sphinx statue
4m × 2m?

Your answers will depend on where you placed the other exhibits.

HOT AND COLD

Heating and cooling a building takes ENERGY. Buildings that use LESS energy are kinder to the environment – and it's even better if the energy is from sources which don't harm the planet.

Using the tips around the page, design a building that can HEAT and COOL itself using as little extra energy as possible.

WAYS TO KEEP ~WARM~

ABSORB HEAT

DARK paints and materials absorb heat better than pale ones.

SOLAR COLLECTORS with water inside absorb heat from the Sun...

...then move hot water around the building through pipes and tanks.

WIND TURBINES spin in the wind to make electricity.

GENERATE YOUR OWN ENERGY TO RUN HEATERS

SOLAR PANELS turn the Sun's energy into electricity.

FLOOR TILES that generate electricity when people step on them.

WAYS TO KEEP
COOL

PLANTS on the roof stop the Sun's rays from warming the building.

KEEP THE HEAT OUT

PALE, SHINY surfaces reflect heat.

SUNSHADES above windows create shade.

WINDOWS and OPENINGS can let air in and out if it's breezy.

LET THE BREEZE IN

AIR VENTS pump out warm, stale air.

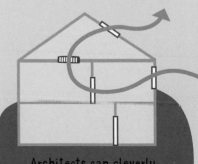

Architects can cleverly place windows, openings and vents so that air is drawn naturally through the building. This is known as PASSIVE VENTILATION.

TINY HOMES

As populations grow, there's less and less SPACE for each person. In some places, such as Tokyo and Hong Kong, this has led to a growing number of teeny houses called TINY HOMES, or MICROHOMES.

Tiny homes can be built in...

...beach huts.

...shipping containers.

...alleyways.

The growing interest in tiny homes has become known as the SMALL-HOUSE MOVEMENT. Tiny homes are good for the environment as they require fewer resources to build and run.

...sheds.

A tiny home includes EVERYTHING you need, cleverly SQUEEZED into as little space as possible.

LAYERS and LEVELS can help to make best use of space.

Windows

Lights

Storage space

Bed

TV

Chairs or sofas

Stove

Toilet

Shower

Sink

Fridge

IMAGINE an architect is building a tiny home in this alleyway. Add an outline, and scribble in everything you think it should contain.

How can you create space to fit everything?

An outdoor shower?

A bed that can fold up against the wall?

A floor that lifts up to store things?

A fold-out TV?

A garden on the roof?

A raised bed...

Purrr

...with a fold-out table underneath?

A ladder instead of stairs?

BUILDING UP

With more and more people living and working in cities, one way to make space is to BUILD UP. But tall buildings can be a challenge for architects...

The taller the building, the greater the risk it might...

...tip...

...sink into the ground...

...or bend out of shape.

Architects make models to TEST their designs. Try it yourself. Make a model building using scrap paper and tape. See how TALL you can make it.

Try these ideas, or come up with your own.

You could roll paper tightly to make TUBES.

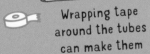

Wrapping tape around the tubes can make them stronger.

Adding CROSS PIECES makes structures more sturdy.

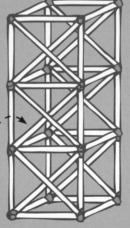

You could roll paper into COLUMNS to support flat floors.

Having more weight at the bottom makes a building less likely to fall over.

You could try to make towering structures from TRIANGLES.

Fold a sheet of paper in half lengthways.

Then, fold it twice to make a triangle...

...and tape the ends together.

Stack your triangles, taping the edges to secure them in place.

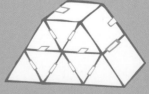
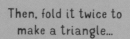

Once you're happy with your building, it's time to TEST it.

SKETCH
your finished model.

Measure the HEIGHT.
How tall is it?

Does it stand up STRAIGHT,
or does it TIP to one side?

Straight / Tips

Test it for WIND RESISTANCE.
Place the building upright
and wave this book at it.
How easy is it to make your
building WOBBLE?

Easy / Not very easy / Hard

Test it for STRENGTH.
Place this book on top of it.
Can it support the weight
without crumpling?

Yes / No

Give your
building a name.

GETTING LOST

In 16th-century Europe, mazes made by growing hedges were a popular form of entertainment. Landscape architects often designed them as part of formal gardens and parks.

Here's one method landscape architects can use to design mazes...

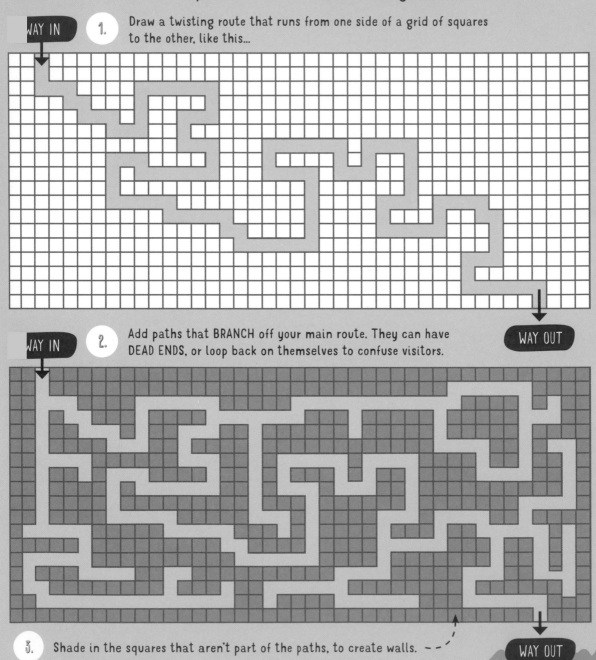

WAY IN

1. Draw a twisting route that runs from one side of a grid of squares to the other, like this...

WAY OUT

WAY IN

2. Add paths that BRANCH off your main route. They can have DEAD ENDS, or loop back on themselves to confuse visitors.

3. Shade in the squares that aren't part of the paths, to create walls. - - -

WAY OUT

DESIGN YOUR OWN hedge maze for this grand garden. Use the grid below.

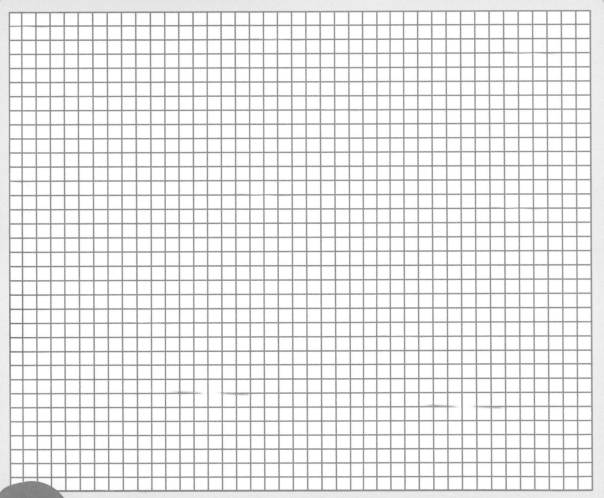

I'm lost!

Make sure you leave gaps to get in and out.

Some architects design buildings that are totally TRANSPORTABLE, so they can be moved from one spot to another.

DESIGN YOUR OWN moveable building. Think about WHY it needs to move, and HOW you would get it from one place to another. There are some real-life examples below.

WHAT: Motor homes
WHERE: All over the world
HOW: Has an engine and wheels
WHY: To move around and see different places

WHAT: The Halley Research Station
WHERE: Antarctica
HOW: Each section can be dragged across the ice by trucks
WHY: To escape cracking ice sheets

To escape
disasters?

**WHY DOES IT NEED
TO MOVE?**

To explore?

To move with
the seasons?

Floats on water?

Picked up by
a crane?

**HOW DOES
IT MOVE?**

Drives along
on wheels?

Pulled along by
a helicopter?

MY MOVEABLE BUILDING

WHAT:

WHERE:

HOW:

WHY:

LIFE IN THE TREES

People have been building and living in tree houses for thousands of years.

Tree houses need to be built in a way that doesn't harm the living trees.

Zzz

Tree houses are usually built around the TRUNK of a tree, and use the sturdiest branches for support.

Some tree houses are built across several trees, with WALKWAYS to connect them.

Most tree houses are made of WOOD, to blend in with their surroundings.

SCREWING INTO a tree can damage it, so it's better to fix things AROUND the tree, pushing AGAINST the wood.

BRACKETS like this can be added for strength.

To get up and down, you could use a ladder, or a PULLEY system.

HEAVE HO!

STILTS help to support the weight.

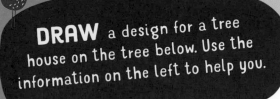

DRAW a design for a tree house on the tree below. Use the information on the left to help you.

WALL PATTERNS

Around 800 years ago, some architects in parts of Asia and Africa began decorating buildings with vibrant designs known as GIRIH PATTERNS (pronounced "girry" patterns).

Architects mapped out their patterns using five shapes (numbered 1-5 here). Each shape had a set arrangement of lines on top.

The five shapes are known as GIRIH TILES.

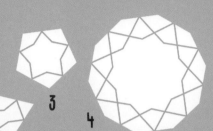

1

2

3

4

5

If you fit the white shapes together – all of them or just some of them – the lines create a pattern. This is known as a GIRIH PATTERN.

Different arrangements make different girih patterns.

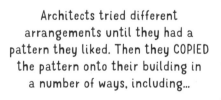

Architects tried different arrangements until they had a pattern they liked. Then they COPIED the pattern onto their building in a number of ways, including...

...CARVING it into stone walls...

...or arranging glazed TILES.

Girih patterns were often added to MOSQUES and other Islamic buildings.

TRY IT YOURSELF

Copy this template, or print it from Usborne QUICKLINKS. Then follow the instructions below to create your own GIRIH PATTERN.

Copy or print it as many times as you want until you have enough girih tiles to make your pattern.

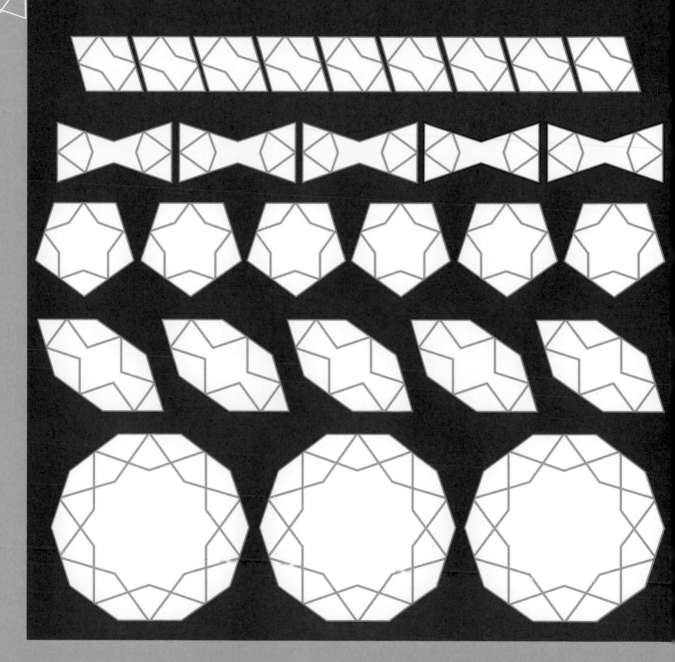

 1 Cut out your girih tiles along the blue lines. Then try fitting them together in different ways.

 2 Once you have a pattern you like, draw it or stick it down on the building on the next page.

YOUR
MASTERPIECE

Draw or stick down your girih pattern
in the space below. Then fill it in to
make it bright, bold and vibrant.

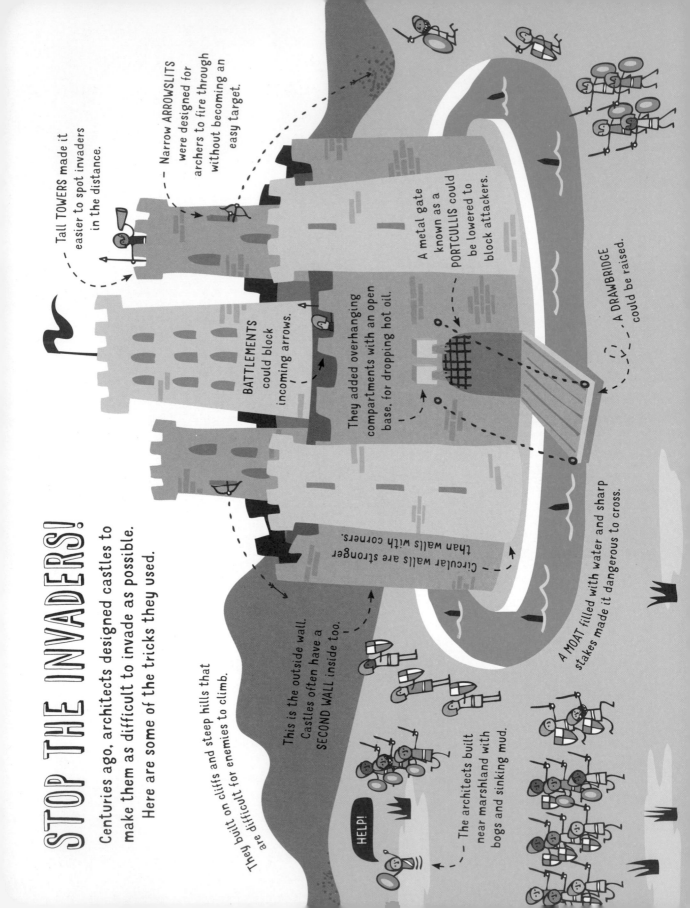

STOP THE INVADERS!

Centuries ago, architects designed castles to make them as difficult to invade as possible. Here are some of the tricks they used.

Tall TOWERS made it easier to spot invaders in the distance.

Narrow ARROWSLITS were designed for archers to fire through without becoming an easy target.

A metal gate known as a PORTCULLIS could be lowered to block attackers.

BATTLEMENTS could block incoming arrows.

They added overhanging compartments with an open base, for dropping hot oil.

Circular walls are stronger than walls with corners.

A DRAWBRIDGE could be raised.

A MOAT filled with water and sharp stakes made it dangerous to cross.

They built on cliffs and steep hills that are difficult for enemies to climb.

This is the outside wall. Castles often have a SECOND WALL inside too.

The architects built near marshland with bogs and sinking mud.

HELP!

CHAAAARGE!

DESIGN a castle SECURE enough to survive an attack by fierce invaders. Use the ideas above to inspire you.

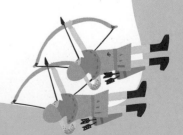

SECRET GARDENS

A secret garden is a place that's hidden from the rest of the world, making a calm, peaceful space for people to relax in.

Think about what YOU would want in YOUR secret garden, and scribble your ideas below. There are suggestions around the page to help you.

Perches for singing birds?

What might make your secret garden relaxing?

A rose garden?

On an island in a lake?

Where would you hide your secret garden?

Tucked away on a rooftop?

Sheltered behind trees?

MY SECRET GARDEN

HIDDEN LOCATION:

SECRET ENTRANCE:

FEATURES:

An octopus-shaped fountain?

What features could your garden have?

A hedge maze?

A cactus garden?

A hidden door that opens with a motion sensor?

Disguised to look like a tree?

How could you disguise the entrance?

A wooden archway covered in hanging ivy?

SCRIBBLE a design for your secret garden.

You could draw a BUBBLE DIAGRAM (see page 22)... (see page 22)

Building

...or create a plan using SYMBOLS (see page 23)... (see page 23)

Tree

Flowerbed

Bench

...or do a two-minute sketch (see page 9). (see page 9)

KNOCKING DOWN WALLS

Most buildings will stay standing even if you REMOVE some of the walls. But LOAD-BEARING WALLS carry the weight of the building. If you remove them, the building will COLLAPSE, unless you add extra support elsewhere.

In this floorplan, the load-bearing walls are shown in black.

This plan only shows the layout of the WALLS. Extra supports in the floors and ceilings, known as BEAMS and JOISTS, help to keep the building standing too.

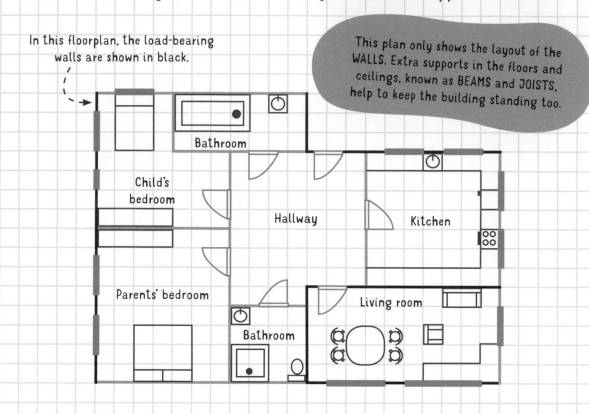

Bathroom

Child's bedroom

Hallway

Kitchen

Parents' bedroom

Bathroom

Living room

The family living in the house above wants to make some changes...

Make the kitchen and living room one BIG room.

Add another bedroom for when friends and family stay over.

Add a bathroom with a bathtub joined to our bedroom.

Make my bedroom bigger!

REDESIGN the floorplan to meet the family's requests.

The load-bearing walls have to stay in the same place, but you can move or remove the other walls, and add as many new ones as you like.

You can change what each room is used for, and you can rearrange the symbols.

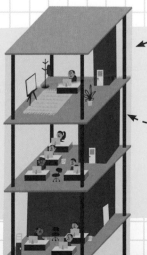

When a building's OUTSIDE walls DON'T carry any of the weight, the outer wall is known as a CURTAIN WALL. This building has a glass curtain wall.

Curtain wall

The load-bearing walls (shown in pink) are on the inside.

Columns carry some of the weight, too.

The curtain wall shields the load-bearing walls. If harsh weather damages the curtain wall, the building will stay standing because the load-bearing walls are protected.

LOOKALIKES

By creatively arranging and shaping walls, windows, doors and roofs, architects can design buildings that resemble other things.

DESIGN YOUR OWN
Pick an object, and design a building that looks similar to it. There are some examples around the page to give you ideas.

NAME AND LOCATION: The Autohaus, Austria
DESIGNED BY: Markus Voglreiter
LOOKS LIKE: A car

NAME AND LOCATION: Burj Al Arab Jumeirah, Dubai
DESIGNED BY: Tom Wright
LOOKS LIKE: A boat's sail

LOOKALIKE QUIZ

What do these
buildings resemble?

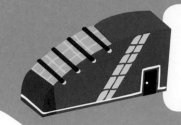

LOOKS LIKE:

LOOKS LIKE:

MY LOOKALIKE BUILDING

BUILDING NAME:

DESIGNED BY:

LOOKS LIKE:

BRIDGES

Architects work with engineers to create BRIDGES that are not only strong, safe and long-lasting, but also striking and interesting to look at.

Here are the basic structures for three different bridge types:

ARCH BRIDGES are the simplest type of bridge.

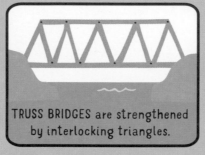

TRUSS BRIDGES are strengthened by interlocking triangles.

SUSPENSION BRIDGES use cables to support their weight.

Architects can add features to these basic structures to create a striking design.

Decorative supports?

Pick a type of bridge, draw the basic structure below and **SCRIBBLE** a design on top.

Castle turrets?

Plants?

A NEW USE

Humans create billions of tons of WASTE each year. Architects can help to reduce that amount by REUSING available waste in their buildings.

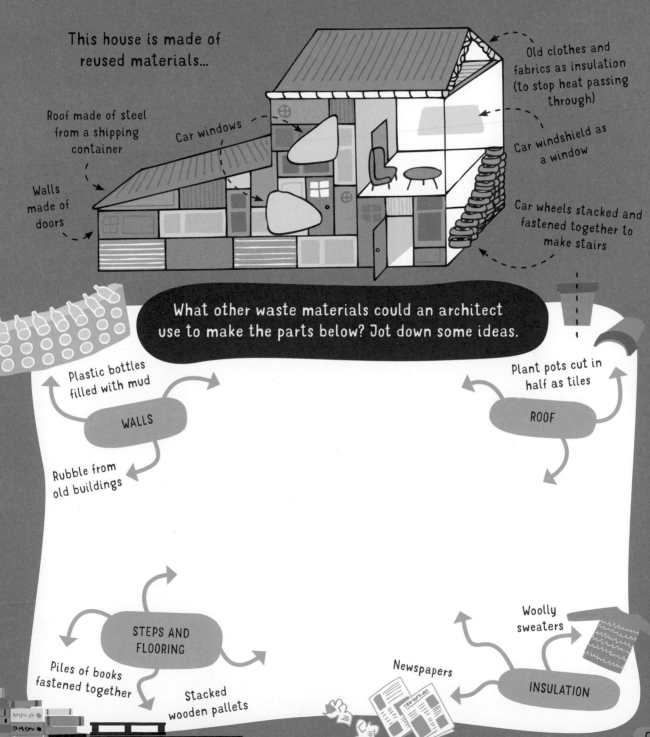

This house is made of reused materials...

Old clothes and fabrics as insulation (to stop heat passing through)

Roof made of steel from a shipping container

Car windows

Car windshield as a window

Walls made of doors

Car wheels stacked and fastened together to make stairs

What other waste materials could an architect use to make the parts below? Jot down some ideas.

Plastic bottles filled with mud

Plant pots cut in half as tiles

WALLS

ROOF

Rubble from old buildings

STEPS AND FLOORING

Woolly sweaters

Piles of books fastened together

Newspapers

Stacked wooden pallets

INSULATION

SHAKY GROUND

When an EARTHQUAKE strikes, buildings shake, and sometimes COLLAPSE. But there are several clever techniques that architects can use to help to keep structures standing.

Pendulum ← Building →

A PENDULUM

can be hung on the top of a building. In an earthquake, the pendulum swings in the opposite direction to the building, BALANCING it.

A FLEXIBLE FRAME

allows a structure to BEND as the ground shakes. Wood and steel are flexible, but concrete and stone frames are brittle and likely to crumble.

DIAGONAL BRACING

helps to reinforce the frame and make it STRONGER.

SHOCK ABSORBERS

can be fitted between a building and its FOUNDATION. They shake with the earthquake, but stop the movement from going further up the building.

Foundation

MAKE IT SAFE

This skyscraper is going to be built in a region at risk of earthquakes. Scribble in some features to make it safer.

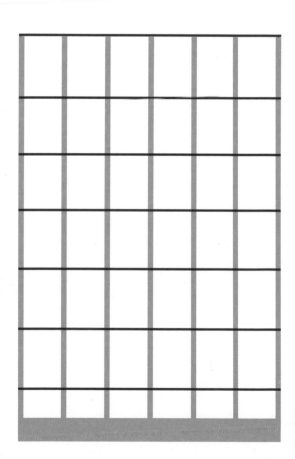

Frame material:

Shade a star for each safety feature you add.

BUILDING UNDERGROUND

Some spots, such as steep hillsides or areas prone to extreme weather, aren't good for ordinary houses. In these areas, often the answer is to go UNDERGROUND.

WHY GO UNDERGROUND?

Earth makes great INSULATION. It helps to keep buildings WARM in winter and COOL in summer.

Buildings surrounded by earth are more SOUNDPROOF.

Undergound buildings don't need foundations. This makes them CHEAPER to build.

DESIGN YOUR OWN
underground house.

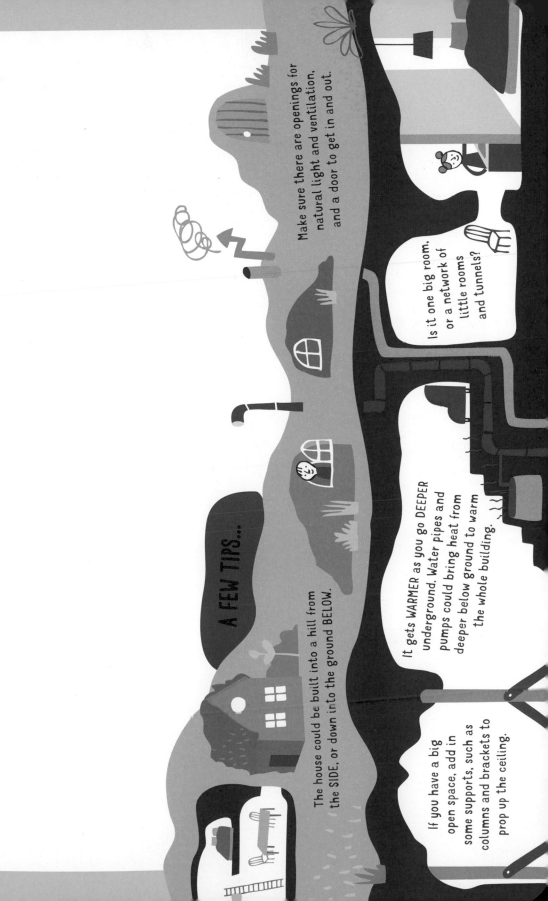

Make sure there are openings for natural light and ventilation, and a door to get in and out.

Is it one big room, or a network of little rooms and tunnels?

A FEW TIPS...

The house could be built into a hill from the SIDE, or down into the ground BELOW.

It gets WARMER as you go DEEPER underground. Water pipes and pumps could bring heat from deeper below ground to warm the whole building.

If you have a big open space, add in some supports, such as columns and brackets to prop up the ceiling.

ARTIFICIAL ISLANDS

Because the number of people in the world is going up, and sea levels are rising, the demand for land is growing. One solution is to create completely new land by building ARTIFICIAL ISLANDS in the sea.

Building an island can be a tricky business. When architects start thinking about a location, they have lots of things to consider...

Could a new island harm wildlife living nearby?

Is the seabed solid enough to support the weight?

Is the area often hit by bad weather or large waves?

How deep is the water? Too deep and it won't be possible to build a foundation.

Too deep?

On the map below, mark out a suitable area for building an artificial island.

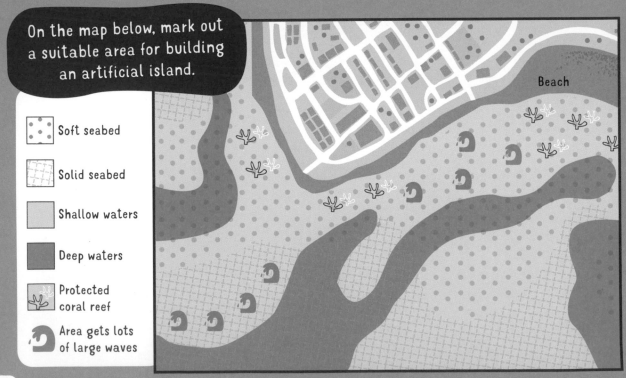

Beach

Soft seabed

Solid seabed

Shallow waters

Deep waters

Protected coral reef

Area gets lots of large waves

Artificial islands come in lots of shapes and sizes, depending on what they've been built for.

The Palm Islands in Dubai resemble a gigantic palm tree when seen from the air. They are used for luxury hotels and homes.

This long, rectangular island was built to house Kansai International Airport in Japan.

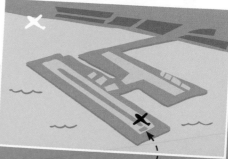

RUNWAY for planes to take off

DESIGN YOUR OWN
artificial island.

Could it be a star-shaped luxury resort?

Or an oval shape for a race track?

Will there be a town - and if so, what buildings will it have?

A hospital?

A school?

Houses and shops?

How will people reach the island? By bridge? Or could there be a dock for boats?

BUILDING FOR EVERYONE

Part of an architect's job is to make a building ACCESSIBLE.
That means making it easy for EVERYBODY to use, regardless
of their physical ability, age, size or language.

Look at the visitors below, then write or
draw features you would add to meet their
needs. Use the suggestions at the bottom of
the page, or come up with your own ideas.

I can't find the way
out. I don't speak
English!

The door is too
narrow for my
scooter...

I can't see.
How do I work out
where I am?

The stairs are
too steep – I need
something to hold.

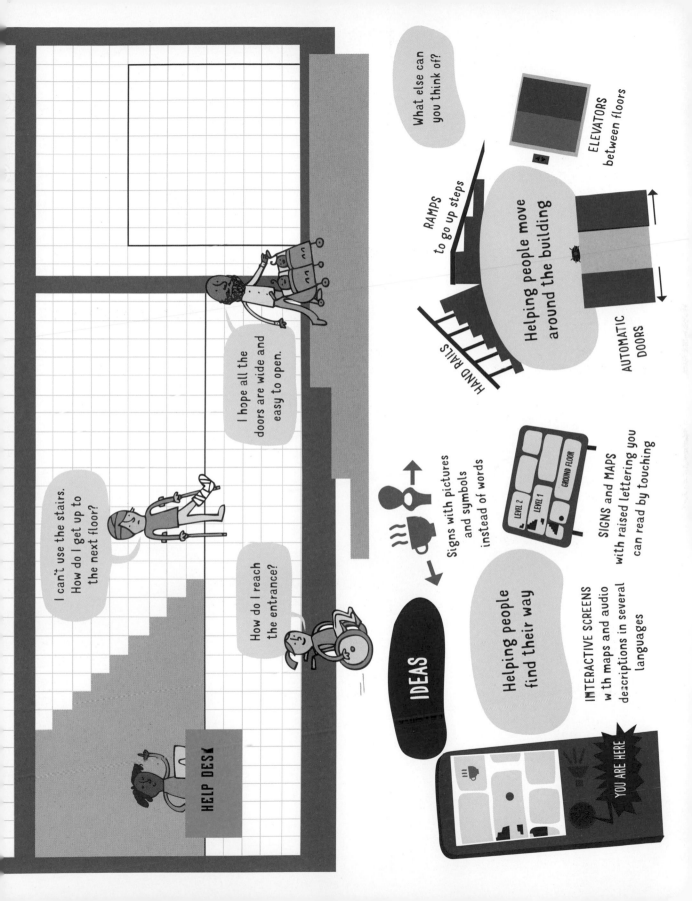

MAKING MODELS

As part of the design process, architects often make
SCALE MODELS of a building and its surroundings.

They use the models to test
out different ARRANGEMENTS...

FRONT

...to examine the
building from different
VIEWPOINTS...

SIDE 1

SIDE 2

...and to work out where
there will be SHADE when lit
from different angles.

BUILD A MODEL CAFÉ

Use the template on the next page to
design a park café. Then follow the
instructions to make it into a model.

Copy the template,
or print it from
Usborne QUICKLINKS.

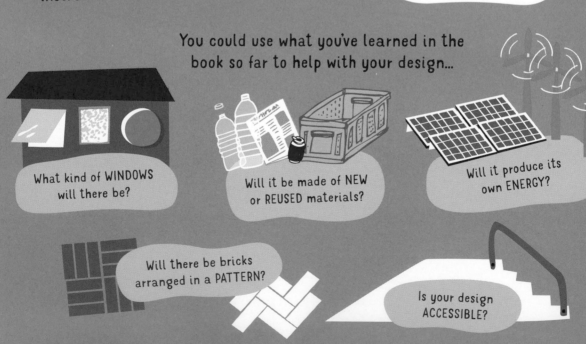

You could use what you've learned in the
book so far to help with your design...

What kind of WINDOWS
will there be?

Will it be made of NEW
or REUSED materials?

Will it produce its
own ENERGY?

Will there be bricks
arranged in a PATTERN?

Is your design
ACCESSIBLE?

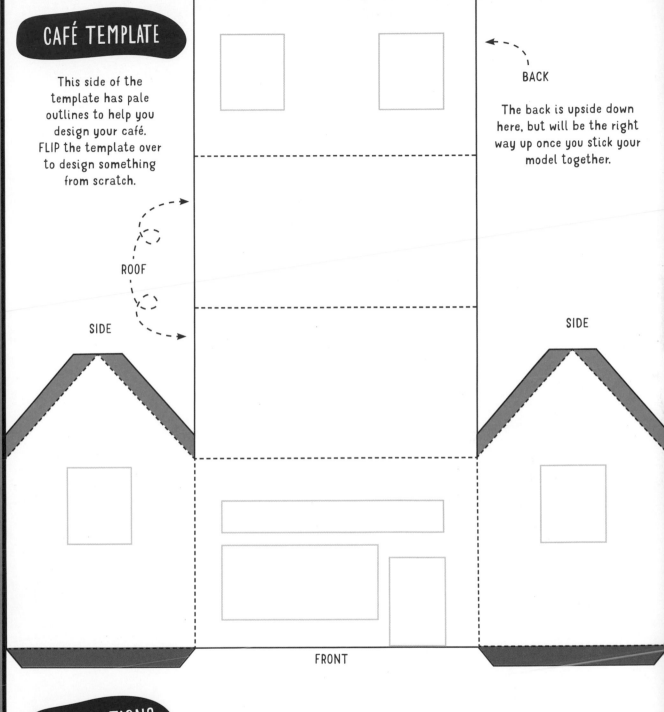

CAFÉ TEMPLATE

This side of the template has pale outlines to help you design your café. FLIP the template over to design something from scratch.

ROOF

SIDE

BACK

The back is upside down here, but will be the right way up once you stick your model together.

SIDE

FRONT

INSTRUCTIONS

1.
Cut along the SOLID BLACK lines.

2.
Fold along the DOTTED lines to make a building shape, with your design on the outside.

3.
Stick the BLUE tabs onto the inside, to hold the model together.

Turn the page for the next part of the task.

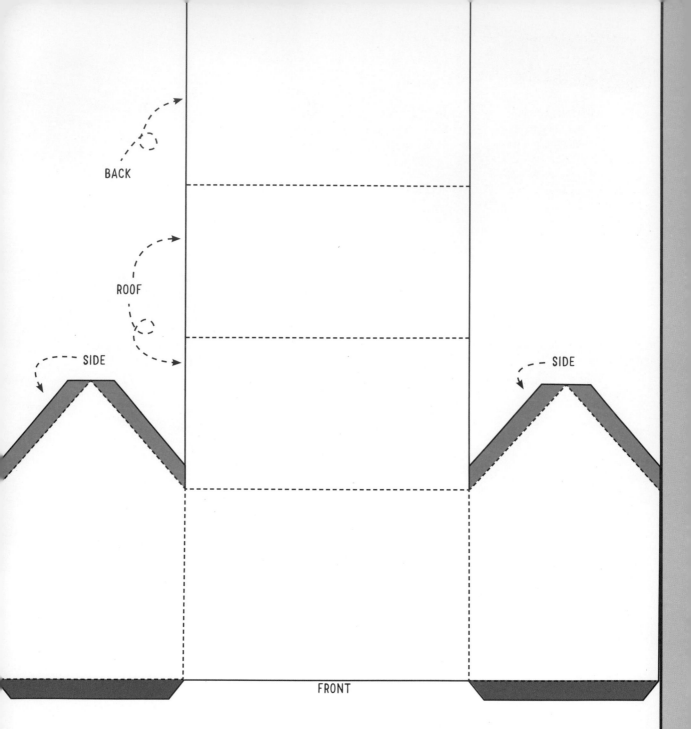

BACK

ROOF

SIDE

SIDE

FRONT

DESIGN THE PARK

Copy the template below, or print it from Usborne QUICKLINKS. Mark on the template where you will put your model, DESIGN the park around it, then STICK DOWN your model using the PURPLE tabs.

You could add...

...a pond?

...a café veggie patch?

...a secret garden?

What else?

PARK TEMPLATE

Use the outlines on this side of the template to start off your design, or flip it over to design from scratch.

Which side of the café will get the most sunlight?

WORKING WITH THE PAST

Architects don't always design COMPLETELY new buildings – sometimes they create new spaces using buildings that are ALREADY THERE, but no longer used for their old role. This is known as ADAPTIVE REUSE. It keeps the building's historic style intact.

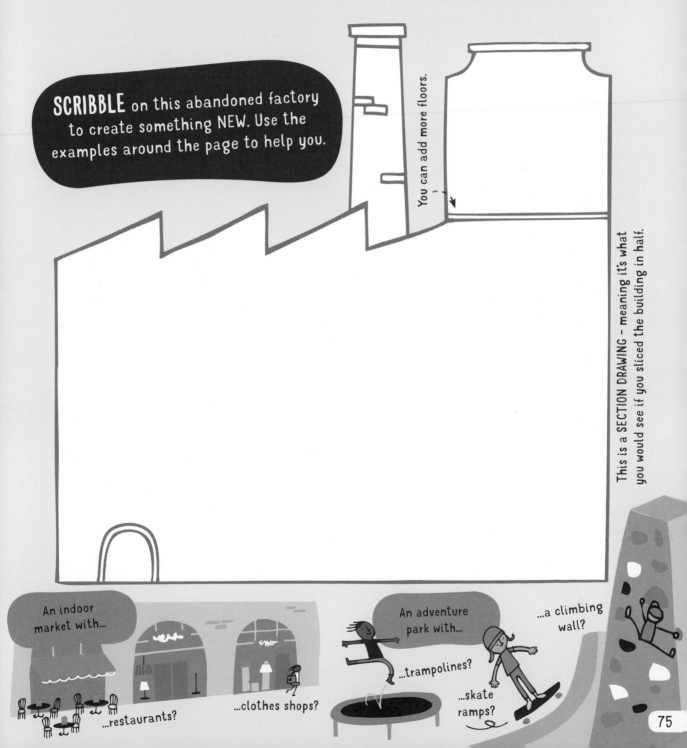

SCRIBBLE on this abandoned factory to create something NEW. Use the examples around the page to help you.

You can add more floors.

This is a SECTION DRAWING – meaning it's what you would see if you sliced the building in half.

An indoor market with...

...restaurants?

...clothes shops?

An adventure park with...

...trampolines?

...skate ramps?

...a climbing wall?

WHAT'S IMPORTANT?

Different architects can have very different opinions about what buildings should be like. Some publish their ideas in a document known as a MANIFESTO. Answer the questions below to help you write YOUR OWN manifesto.

What would you rather build? CIRCLE the options you prefer.

A building with intricate, bright DECORATION

OR

A building with SIMPLE SHAPES and not much decoration

A building that BLENDS IN with buildings nearby

OR

A building that STANDS OUT and looks different

A LUXURY building that spares no expense

OR

A modest building that doesn't harm the environment

Can you think of any things you **DON'T** like about buildings you've seen? Note things to AVOID here.

Rooms without many windows?

Particular materials, such as wood or marble?

> Talk about beauty and you get boring answers, but talk about ugliness and things get interesting.

Dutch architect Rem Koolhaas (born 1944)

How should a building make people inside **FEEL?** Scribble some ideas.

Safe?

Comfortable?

INSPIRED?

WELCOME?

Architecture is really about well-being. I think people want to feel good in a space.

Iraqi-British architect
Zaha Hadid
(1950-2016)

Now you've thought through some ideas, write your manifesto here.

MY ARCHITECTURE MANIFESTO

The buildings I design **WILL...**

My buildings **WON'T...**

Good buildings should make people **FEEL...**

DREAM HOME

Use the architecture skills you've developed in this book to design your own DREAM HOME.

There are some suggestions around the page to help you.

Where would it be?

Out in space?

Up a mountain?

On an ordinary street?

Underwater?

What features would it have?

Rooftop pool?

A room for watching movies?

Space for all your friends or pets?

Underground rooms?

Wahoo!

Slides to take you downstairs?

Living trees?

Bricks made
of gold?

**What materials
would you use?**

Shells?

Stained glass?

French mailman Ferdinand
Cheval began building his dream
house in 1879 in his garden.

He collected stones while delivering mail,
then arranged them into this intricate palace.
It took him 33 years to finish!

ANSWERS

16-17 STRIKING STYLES

A. Romanesque   **B.** Gothic   **C.** Rococo
D. Classical   **E.** Modernist

21 ICY DOMES

A - 2   B - 1   C - 4   D - 3   E - 5

26-27 RESTORATIONS

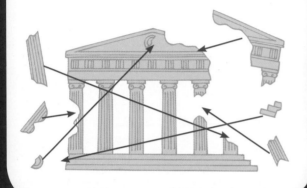

32-33 FLOOD ZONE

Crab Street - 1   Cliffside Way - 3
Pebble Road - 2

34-35 SCALE DRAWINGS

PURPLE WALL=1.5m / 150cm   CROWN=21cm
ORANGE WALL=8m / 800cm   SPACESUIT=170cm

58-59 LOOKALIKES

SHOE   DOG

66-67 ARTIFICIAL ISLANDS

 Anywhere on the map with this background and shade of blue would be suitable for an artificial island.

Photographic credits: P.79 - Ferdinand Cheval's dream home © Milosk50/Dreamstime.com.

Additional expert advice from Dr. Peter Lu, Harvard University

Additional content by Alice James and Sarah Hull   Additional design by Laura Bridges